# WILDLIFE IN THE OCEANS AND SEAS FOR KIDS
## (Aquatic & Marine Life)
## 2nd Grade Science Edition Vol 6

Speedy Publishing LLC
40 E. Main St. #1156
Newark, DE 19711
www.speedypublishing.com

Oceans contain the greatest diversity of life on Earth.

The killer
whale is a
toothed whale
belonging to
the oceanic
dolphin family.
They prey
on seals, sea
lions, fish, sea
birds, turtles,
octopuses,
and squid.

Killer whales have the second largest brain of all marine mammals.

Clownfish have a symbiotic relationship with sea anemone which is a fish-eating plant-like animal that has poisonous tentacles.

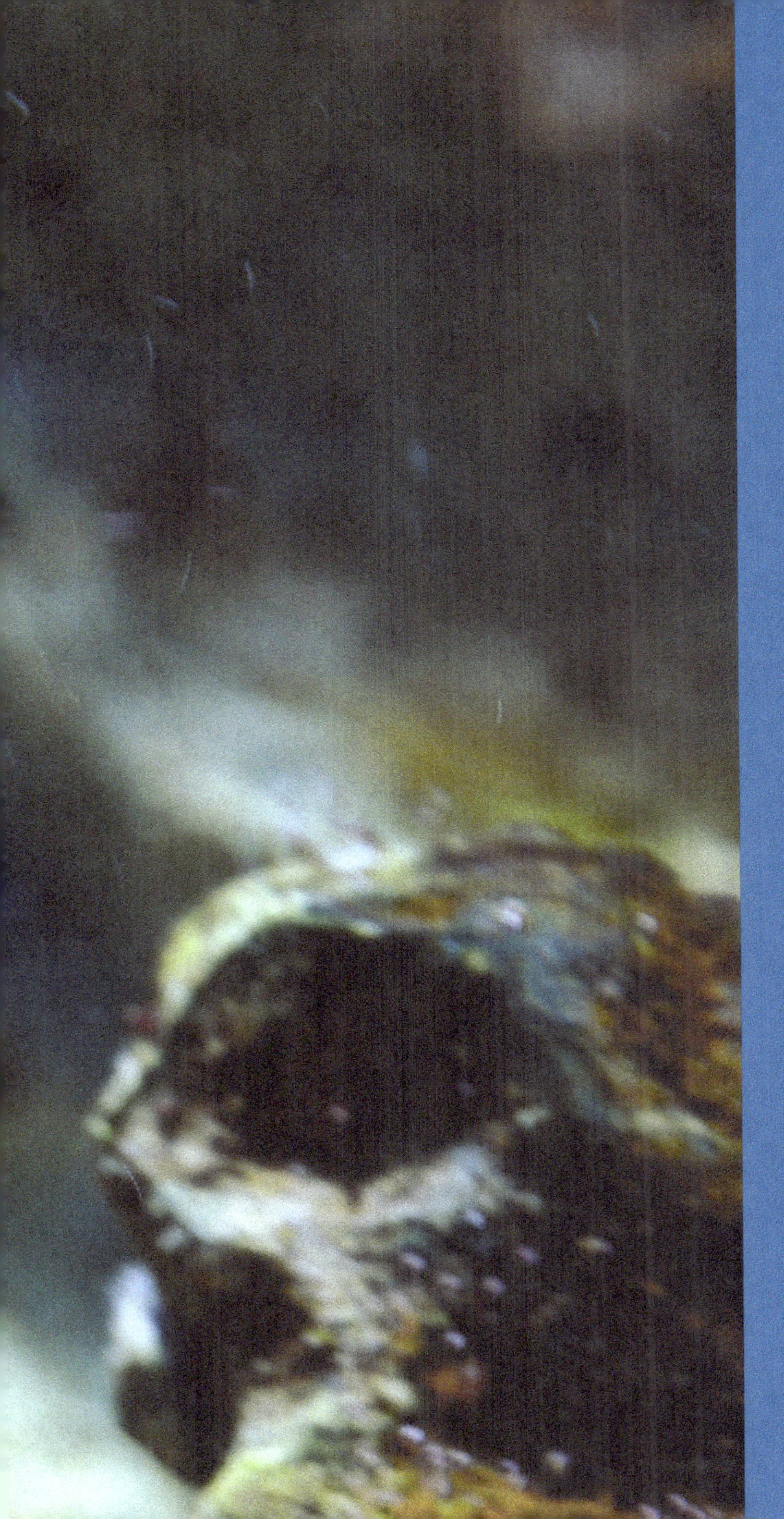

Clownfish
are found in
warm waters
of the Indian
and Pacific
Oceans.

Bottlenose dolphins are known for their short, thick beaks. Bottlenose dolphins have been known to interact with humans.

Bottlenose dolphin sleep with one eye open and the other closed. When the left brain sleeps, the right eye is closed and when the right half sleeps the left eye is closed.

Green Sea Turtle - named for the green color of the fat under its shell. Adult Green Turtles grow to 1.5 meters long.

The green
sea turtle
juveniles are
omnivorous,
but as they
mature they
become
exclusively
herbivorous.

Cuttlefish belong to the same class as squid, octopuses and the nautilus.

Cuttlefish are sometimes called the chameleon of the sea because they are able to change their skin color.

The great
white sharks
are the
world's
largest
predatory
fish, with
mature
individuals
growing up
to 6.4 meters
in length.

Great White Sharks have excellent sense of smell, they can smell one drop of blood in a million drops of water.

Manta rays are the largest rays. Manta Rays are generally found in warm waters across the planet.

Manta rays have the largest brain to body weight ratio of any living fish.

Manatees
are large,
fully aquatic,
mostly
herbivorous
marine
mammals.

Manatees
are slow
swimmers.
They usually
swim between
3-5 miles
per hour.

Seahorses
are fish.
They live in
water, breath
through gills
and have a
swim bladder.

Male seahorses have a pouch on the front side of their body. When female deposits her eggs inside the pouch, male fertilizes them internally.

Visit
BABY PROFESSOR
EDUCATION KIDS
www.BabyProfessorBooks.com
to download Free Baby Professor eBooks
and view our catalog of new and exciting
Children's Books